Line Study of a Motel Clerk

Line Study of a Motel Clerk

Allison Pitinii Davis

BAOBAB PRESS
RED OCHRE EDITION

First Printing

17   18   19   20   21

10   9   8   7   6   5   4   3   2   1

ISBN-13: 978-1-936097-13-5

ISBN-10: 1-936097-13-3

Library of Congress Control Number: 2016941514

Red Ochre Edition, an imprint of Baobab Press

121 California Avenue

Reno, Nevada 89509

www.baobabpress.com

Cover Design by Travis Bennett

Cover Image courtesy of Allison Pitinii Davis

Printed in the United States of America

To Linda and Murray Davis, Rhoda and Bill Davis,
and Betty and Mike Pitinii

Contents

The 1970s

Migrations

The Long Turn

The Great Bearer of Keys

The 1970s

In the Back of the Motel Clerk's Mind, the Key Rack

There is a way to love things open,
to turn and turn:

a line of numbered doors hinging
on the highway.

There is a June night thickening with duplicates.

There is a spare geometry of vacancy.

There are the keys. They hang like filthy bats
chiming on the hour. Oh Pall Mall tower,

their teeth are sharp! Nocturnal with cavity.

They are enough to make money.
To make nervous.

On the rack, each hook sags
rich with understudies,

perfect copies
cut out

for their work.

The Motel Clerk's Son Writes His Lover's Name on the Marquee

in black block letters above the words
COLD BEER. The ladder shakes
with each passing semi. Bracing himself

on the sign, he finishes her last name,
running out of *I*s
and switching to *l*s. Back in the office,

he stares at her name
ruling the turnpike exit like a queen.
He's watching Friday's traffic for her car

when a trucker arrives, grabs a Genesee
from the cooler, and sets it on the counter
beside the bell. Her Camaro pulls in

to the lot. *Hell this one's*
on me he says, trying
to clear out the office. The trucker slams

cash on the counter and says, *kid, you trying*
to run your old man's business
into the ground?

On the Drive to the Motel, Sohios

recede in the side mirrors of her Camaro. Coors neons flick on
down the strip. This morning she lit a candle
at St. Demetrious. Above her stretch garlands
of tandem phone wires. Her eyeliner's drawn

by her sisters, her sisters drawn to the car plant,
the car plant full of money to take home.
Where never is heard a discouraging word
above the industrial drone.

She parks the car and crosses
the lot alone. In the grey of Ohio
and the gold
she pulls her coat around her in the cold.

A maid ashes a cigarette in greeting.
It's Friday. The city's engines rev and roam.

Greetings from Across the Counter

Generation after generation wake up and worry about business
—on my father's side, a trucking motel; my mother's side, a laun-
dry. Of my parents, people asked, "Why's that Pitinii girl marry-
ing a Jew?" and vice versa. I'm their firstborn: I'll tell you why
they married. My mother woke up asking, "Starch or no starch?"
and my father answered, "Smoking room or non?"

The Motel Clerk's Son Falls in Love While Buildings Fall

The days are short. His beard is Wolfman-length
        for Halloween. The screen door creaks
                as truckers enter and squint

beneath fluorescents, their pupils enlarged
        with Midwest night. Keys change hands
                across the counter,

but she's looking out the window,
        the reflection of her lipstick
                blurring with moon-streaked gas prices

across the street. It's Saturday: they're waiting
        for the night clerk's headlights
                to arc the lot, waiting

to drive through
        the South Side
                harsh with stars

like a grainy midcentury sci-fi
        that starts with a couple
                necking in a car

and ends in a city where everything's over,
        where mothers yell at buildings to fall
                already and stop complaining.

Swings, 1970

The news knifes out
as he drops back-first toward earth: *the Beatles
            broke up*. The news spreads down

the line of swings, lengthening
and collapsing, pumping gravity out
            and in. The playground is 9,000 miles

from Vietnam and 200,000 miles below
Apollo 13. My father is fifteen years away
            from being my father,

my father who heels the gravel
and jerks the chains, roughly halting
            eleven years of his body. In the Ohio afternoon,

robins chirp for what
from budding maples. For what
            my father joins the forming

line behind his room number
painted yellow on the blacktop.
            A noise is building louder

than the mills, unmanned
and tethered
            to nothing, pressing

like a headline
into language, like a fever
            into a nurse's hand. Across town

at Niles McKinley, my mother's sisters
are crying, their coarse hair flat
            after a morning

fanning it over the board
beneath their mother's iron.
      Here is the ending to what started

the night their father
couldn't get any peace
      because six daughters guarded the carpet

around the screaming
girls on Sullivan, the screaming
      guarding the music so closely

that guards were hired
to guard it, the music that asked too much
      and now finally gets it, the screaming light years

away from its cause,
which already swallowed mouthfuls of static
      by the time it hits the ear.

Sound Check, 1979

I knew I was approaching the vibration of the steel building.
—Nikola Tesla

The doorman lights his first Camel. The bartender primps
his afro in the mirror. All along the river,
the mills are closing. The singer approaches
the mike and, because he's from Youngstown,
thanks the fans. Because who knew if someone
would like him? Because here he's safe to remove
his babička's crucifix and prostrate himself
to the gutter, to smear his chest with Vaseline
and glitter, to admit he only likes donuts
sold by angry people, by his diaspora
sick of selling lotto tickets, otherwise who wants
all that artificial maple
ringing in their molars? Because he'd never had real maple,
when first confronted with it
he rubbed his mouth on the tree bark until
his lips bled. Until fans cheered. Until mothers covered
their daughters' eyes, but the daughters,
because they're from Youngstown, thrive
in darkness. They were born with perfect pitch
in a cloud of soot. They never needed to see things
to believe them. They know what's about to happen
to their city. When the singer thanks them,
they say "You're welcome"
with the frequency of demolition.

"Do we have any rock and rollers out there tonight?"

is the first question   the singer swinging it
            like blood through the lion's mouth
                        adjusting his crotch through
                                    pantyhose   his day job

regulation autoworker   the microphone
            up against his tongue   the crowd
                        drunk in the downtown
                                    of '79   my father   everyone

considering what they are out there   tonight each Saturday night
            coming down West Federal
                        stoned dumb on Youngstown Brown
                                    dumb sweet on downtown traffic

past old theaters queued   for demolition   grand balconies
            segregating
                        question   from question
                                    to which the speaker adds another

then ignites it in a fit   of midnight arson   belts it with bouquets
            of beer and time cards   does it
                        while the room is still
                                    a room   before the question's spoiled

rotten   he wants an answer
            because he's aware of the terrible
                        acoustics   of his city and the noise
                                    he needs to make   he needs to

The Approach of Water

For four years, the son of the Motel Clerk builds up courage. On the fifth, he puts on the shirt in which he sold the most door-to-door carpet and asks the Laundryman for his daughter's hand. The Laundryman has six daughters. Shalom Aleichem wrote, "When you have seven daughters, you forget to laugh, because seven daughters is serious business." The Laundryman minds his own business, washes the city's shirts so his family can live in America. So a motel clerk can ask his daughter to leave the church. So one minute he can be resting in his La-Z-Boy beneath a bust of Mary's head, and the next, floating in a household swamped with brides.

Actual Afternoons

This is the season the daughters of the city
marry into bad blood and prepare a feast.
But the winter expects too much.
The statue soldier stares across the plaza
at the steel-money mansions
slumping into Wick Avenue. It's held its gaze
since 1870, a gift of Youngstown's women
who "scoured the country for miles around
for milk and cream and eggs" and held
such a bake sale that some of them fainted.
Did they ring around the statue
like bells, did icicles hyphenate branches
like last names to vacant nests.
Understand the city is steel,
both sides of it. There's no way to make it talk,
to avoid the wreck, the tangle of shape
worked up into a point
now falling like Fahrenheit. At record lows,
there's a separate blessing for it, for blocks of widows
who can't be bribed from stoops, who continue
tugging nude knee-highs up cartography.
In the Sunday edition, newsprint brides
show human patience, yet there are actual afternoons
left for them at the bus stop: the old widows
still standing, waking themselves for the waiting.

She Understands More Than She Lets On

Outwardly, everyone makes a fuss
about the Laundryman's daughter's
ring. But she recalls her first kiss:
ten years ago, received on the Greece leg
of a discount trip for college students.
After, she was so overwhelmed
that her nose bled and bled through
all her host's toilet paper. The host didn't know
she knew Greek—she was too shy
to speak it. In English, the host smiled
and said, "It will be okay!" but in Greek
panicked, "I've never seen such bleeding,
and you know, toilet paper isn't cheap—"

The Motel Clerk's Son Steps on the Glass

at his wedding
to recall his people's suffering
during his greatest joy. The stepping
is shorthand: the shortest alphabet
is steepest. A car horn
to tell his ancestors, "I see you,
may my tongue cleave
to the roof of my mouth
should I forget." He sounds out the glass
because, as truckers say
in the office, "If you can't see them,
they can't see you."

The Motel Clerk's Son Drives Out to Check on Business

Before him, stickers fade across the bumper: NOT JUST PEANUTS,
LAST ONE OUT OF TOWN, TURN OFF THE LIGHTS.
The last employer in Youngstown is the weather:
the truck behind him plows grey snow to the roadside
while another truck lays salt. Over and over, the radio says:
"Prevent fuel-line freeze up! You go or Sohio pays the tow."

The radio signal spans the city
now bisected by 680, runs from the West Side
widows prescribed shock treatment
after their husbands fell dead
on the lines to the East Side workers
who trained their white bosses then got the slip.

He pulls into the motel lot. Business is dead:
inside the office, he stares into the weather
hitting the window. A wrecking ball crashed
through the Sohio station across the street.
What's left of it smiles back without its teeth.
He says, "That's what you get for opening your mouth."

Migrations

The Line Moves at the Laundry

Niles, Ohio

A woman from the same place as Pythagoras
ends up in Ohio. If Greece is one point and Ohio another,
what can solve for the distance between them? A laundry counter

right off McKinley. She sits on the counter
singing "Oh Suzy-ah-na!" her shoes banging
4/4 on the siding. Her son muscles through steam,

he pulls shirts hot off the presses. She says the headlines
are 100% cotton. She washes the windows with wads of newsprint
while his customers form a line to the doorway. She greets each one,

"Nice outside!" in good English. I'm a young girl hiding under the counter.
A bricklayer drops off shirts stained Monday through Friday.
He says to my grandfather, "Hello, how's your mother?" I stare at his boots

from under the counter. This is my history: I watch it with subtitles.
My math is off: it's fixed by the uncles. Most of the time
I don't know what is happening. My lines are cut,

but sometimes I'm useful:
she bats her eyes at the bricklayer, points down at me,
and flirts with him: "*That* my sister."

Greetings

Most Russians read poetry like a litany: Mayakovsky reads like a sailor shouting through a
megaphone to another ship in a heavy sea.   —John Berger with Anya Bostock

Your vows were cut with water. Weep later:
        the pacing is important. When everyone looks,
            wave like a shepherd

who shits with his sheep on the empires.
        Wave the flag harder: become like the weather. Relearn
            proportion: treat your boss

like a distant mountain.
        He'll retreat two steps, your freedom
            expanding. Repeat: the love of the future

is a love of projection! "Please," you would say
        if your lungs hit capacity, "I need a new name,
            one without aftermath!" Forget slowly

but surely—shake the hand
        of each hometown statue, leave your losses
            in some other time zone. These are the ordinals:

do you intersect? Here, time is used wisely—it's pulled
        by good horses—and language: please get on
            with it. Aim for someone's face.

Arriving

Limnos, Greece–New Castle, Pennsylvania

His teeth are continental, darkly
split by ocean. On his Merchant Marine
ID, his lips are closed—his English, broken,
breaking against the margins of the sea.

On deck, some sailors joke
in Dutch, others in German. In plain Greek,
he says nothing much. They learn English:
water is water.

They sing *Heave ho! My lads,*
heave ho! It's a long, long
way to go until the sea rots
the bows of their lips,

until the doctor comes in
with his tools
and rebinds each mouth
like an atlas.

Back on land, he sways like a sailor—the new traffic lights,
held at a distance in his eyes,
buoy beneath their wires
above the snowy Pennsylvania streets.

What can a man do
once he talks his way back
to a wilderness? He grows strange to himself
at kitchen tables.

One morning, he hears his wife whisper
his English into a boiling pot
of water. He watches her drift away
to the cabinet of spices.

An Early Morning

Limnos, Greece–New Castle, Pennsylvania

You wake before the children and the boarders
and stand in your kitchen doorway
in your nightgown. Beams of sunlight crack

at the counters and break across the floor.
Your blood goes blackstrap, circles gleam yellow-violet
beneath your eyes. At the counter, you curve

a paring knife around an orange, your thumb flared
against the blade, the fruit's weight rolling
seasick in your palm. Bitter citrus and the linoleum walk

of your feet. You lift the window. Hydrangeas crowd against
the screen of aluminum mesh. Blackbirds snap like oil
hitting a pan: a heated argument

you heard once then forgot,
a teenage bride
crossing the empty architecture

of an ocean. Your husband comes and goes
across the waters, his blood turned
tide. What a match, I think,

to start a stove with.
How you rocked us
so still our inlands swell with sea.

Inheritance

Whatever he did is characterized by meticulously fine and painstaking craftsmanship. . . . In the care and precision of his lines, people and objects retain their own lives.

—Harvey Shapiro on Charles Reznikoff

1. Reznikoff's parents made hats. His lines are tight
as his parent's stitching:
word-word-word-word-word.
Lines to cover a head on a freezing day.

2. My mother is a bookkeeper,
my father is an innkeeper.
I'm a keeper of a language
that won't register under its name.

3. Reznikoff's mother moved to America
and had a son. She wanted to name him Ezekiel
after her father. The doctor said "Call him Charlie,
he'll be grateful."

4. When the thread unravels, run it between your lips.
When there isn't thread, invent separation.
Double knot the end of every truth.

5. Between being horseman
in Czarist Russia
and trading horses
in Chicago, a Jew stopped in England
and grabbed a new name quickly
as a jacket
that we keep handing down
to inherit the sweat.

The Motel Clerk's Mother

Youngstown, Ohio

You don't know us
but we grew up with your furniture:

your luxury kept odd hours
like a boarder in the house.

The old men at temple
call you a businesswoman,

by which they mean,
like us,

you were born here.
By which they mean

the widows from Europe
blackened their gloves

but you were the kind of bitch
who bought a fur

and got the hell out of town.

The Laundryman's Mother

Samos, Greece–Niles, Ohio

> There is music in the spacing of the spheres.
>
> > —Pythagoras

> Who will know what you meant?
>
> > —Louis Zukofsky

I.   Your apron tied in a rage at the hipbones.
On loop without distraction: a girl
stern in an overcast orchard,
her serious mouth stained concord.

You remember beautiful Helen—we were afraid to hug her
because she smoked. Aunt Helen maybe didn't want us
to hug her anyway. Her hair was so black
her own mother once held her head beneath the kitchen faucet
to check for dye. I imagine a hand through her hair,
her ear turned to the drain: a strange mermaid
listening to a seashell in the pipes.

II.   Your son's house, your morning sound:
a knife scraping down burnt toast, a white sink
flecked with ash. Odysseus recruits you
from a mounted plate above the faucet.

When Aunt Helen smoked on the couch,
you sat up straight, pretended to take a drag,
and deadpanned: "The new system."

III.   Silence is expensive—
         the expensive neighborhoods
         are quiet. Saying nothing's beyond
         our means. A cousin filibusters
         in each room we plan on keeping.

         _____

         You're not here, you're halfway down Washington Avenue
         leaning against the car of a neighbor,
         your ankles crossed like a teenage hitchhiker
         far from home.

Arriving in Canada

Dubrova, Poland–Montréal, Canada

I.

When she was a young girl
in Yiddish Québec
with her eyes fixed simply
through snowfall

when her mother bore through sweatshop days
like fortress doorways

when, singing like nothing

the maple leaf
our emblem dear
the maple leaf
forever

when, the branches full of brown birds

II.

When she was a young girl
in Yiddish Québec
her mother got off work
on Yom Kippur

lit Yahrzeit candles for her sisters
left in Europe

then went to the double feature downtown

and with the rest of the sweatshop workers
in their Shabbos best
drifted to sleep then awoke
to a strange moment of Hollywood

flickering before them

The Jewish Cemetery at Youngstown

The Motel Clerk's at one end
of Ohev Tzedek's cemetery
and Sandra Scheuer's at the other. She was shot

walking to class at Kent State. His obituary
headline: "Owned Motel." I didn't know
either of them, my grandma

knew both. We set rocks on their icy graves,
say Kaddish. In "The Jewish Cemetery
at Newport," Longfellow asks what drove each person

across the sea. After the shootings,
Mr. Scheuer said, "We left Germany
to guarantee that our daughters could live

in a country with freedom." Her grave looks like the rest.
I've met her sister, and if I were her,
I'd be sick of people

historicizing my sister, parading her
as I'm parading her, as art
parades things, and for what?

So I can imagine my grandparents
in love: when they fought,
he'd lock himself in the car,

and in full view of the neighbors
she'd pound
on the windshield.

He'd watch her lipsticked
mouth rage silently
on the other side of the glass.

Sandy Scheuer, forgive me: do you remember
my grandmother?
She's the widow standing

in the cold and nothing will shut her
up above the grave
where she's still talking as if he hears her,

as if the ground's an Ohio windshield
her ruby mouth scrapes
to clear of snow.

What It Sounds Like from Here

And what the hell do you mean says your father. With all the blankness in the world
chirps your mother. With all the clocks aiming north
says a cousin. You've got us all wrong sing the dead.
With *Keneder Adler* hot off the presses. With wartime
seriousness. With peddlers shouting "Kalimera,
kalimera!" outside the window.

From the Back Room of the Laundry
Niles, Ohio

His father died young and
his grandfathers were strangers
  across the sea, so it's the smile
  of a Greek tailor

that he describes so carefully
that I can see it:
  this smile pressed
  and sharply folded

by my grandfather
who has outlived everyone
  he wants to talk to
  to the point that I suffice

this afternoon in Niles
in his high-ceilinged laundry
  so full of steam
  that I can barely see him

but it is something
just to barely see a grandfather
  close his eyes
  like the lion before the movies

as his huge head falls
and swings back up
  to some insane summit
  from which he booms

"his smile was something
to see, do you hear me?
  It was something
  to see—"

The Merchant Marine's Daughter

Niles, Ohio

Braids of garlic garland the kitchen
        window. Sun strikes the wall

of mounted plates: Aegean ships, a deer's
wide eyes, Grecian wildflowers
        twisting from their vines. Below them,

lemon skins and tea cups
        dot the table.

When you say
"Those men went where the wind
        carried them—"

your palm resting
        against the table

smooths across the country,
smoothing and smoothing America
        like some long cloth you're pressing at your husband's laundry.

The Long Turn

The Motel Clerk's Granddaughter Restocks the Beer Cooler

Coors Light, Coors Light, Bud: the thud
of one case then another. I'm almost done
when my grandmother walks into the office
from her room upstairs. It's early.
She pours a Styrofoam cup of coffee
and grabs a Hershey bar from its display.
She's about to head back up
when the delivery man returns
with the last case of Genesee. Seeing her
in her housecoat, he says, "Hey, Mrs. D,
look at you!" She poses and fluffs her hair.
The reflection of the sunrise
glints above her in the beer cooler.

Dead Language

Before pulling up a carpet at the motel, my father
points out a faint stain and a snag. Morning light
fills the doorway but he flips on the yellowed bulb
and tells me to look. It looks fine. He shakes his head,
hikes up his jeans, and rips back the baseboard with equal
and opposite joy, wood paneling stripping up with glue.
He rolls the carpet then hoists it up on my shoulder,
grabs the other end then overpaces me, ramming
the carpet forward like a log. It thuds into the dump.
Across the street, red rigs punctuate another Ohio dawn.
In the naked room, tile glue old as Eisenhower
loops a frantic message across the floor.

The Line Speeds Up

His father worked the line, a tanner. *And so*? His father's father owned a mill. It's loud in here. *Louder.* Americani, not a Bubbe or a Yia Yia. Ichele woke fully dressed for the wedding. *They remember*? They got stoned to forget. *Forget what*—a word, I can't say it in writing. With a cigar in all those boxes, with broken glasses. Yidel sold fruit and she asked why aren't you married? Or something like that—I've corrected the spellings—*oh well aren't you educated!* Are you talking to me? *No, Razel Etta!* Well, that changes everything, I've been speaking as Allison. *I was being sarcastic!* So I says to her cover your head when you pray to the union Bow there on which side your dad's side can you even say Kaddish then go to a show? *Who else is talking!* The shoeshine on Swallow. *Do you want to get fired?* You know she loves Walter Pidgeon *faster* a hand *keep moving* GM a night turn a red eye a black eye and *oh say can you* a hazel

Greetings from the End of the Line

"A poet is worth less than a garlic peel,"
says Ravikovitch. You know what we think? We were dots on a cloth
spread across a large table, fixed in a pattern. The table was then swapped out
for something smaller. They fanned out the cloth,
it fell where it may. We were the same
but found ourselves positioned over the edge.
We appealed: we don't come from here;
we have no sense of balance. Didn't we know
there are real problems in this world,
don't we have any manners? Us, they said this to,
who cut letters from our names
when there wasn't enough alphabet
to go around, who scaled back
until we grew lighter
than onion skin, who sold the fringed corners
of our fathers' prayer shawls
and replaced them with our own hair. Now, in the recovery, the large table's been returned.
Our parents ask where we put everything, where did we put the spell
to remove the evil eye? Do we look like historians?
Where do they think poets put a thing
that was such a waste of spit, a waste of evil?

The Motel Clerk's Sons Take Over the Business

"You know the one about your father on Channel 43?
Thirty years ago, when we were in our twenties, VCRs got big
and adult videos came out. So we get the A/B switches
and install them in the rooms—B for cable and A for the porn
that looped every couple of hours. The hotels
up the road got them, it's business,
what can you do? All right—
so 43 comes into the office and says
they want an interview. It's just a reporter,
a cameraman, and your father." The phone rings.
My uncle scribbles down the reservation and jabs it
through a key hook. "So the reporter asks your father,
'Are there complaints about the videos?'
Your father rubs his beard—
he's nervous—looks into the camera
and says, 'Sometimes
customers call the office
and complain that the picture
isn't clear enough.'"

Language Loosened Back

My father swished and spit soap until his father
        heard the language flow deep in Youngstown's sewers.
                Conditioning. My years of speech therapy, my father's—a star
for every *R*. When we visited Montréal, his grandmother served fish
        while asking who I was in Yiddish.
                She slid the fish toward me, eye-first.
I retreated. One theory about why
        the Guard shot at Kent is not "students threw rocks" but
                some "co-eds called Guards motherfucking cocksuckers."
After such language, why separate women from men,
        student from felon? A decade earlier, Lenny Bruce yelled *cocksucker*
                until he was acquitted, until the word didn't separate,
until oil and water got along. I just want to get along, so why'd I tell my father
        to stick his ballot up my cunt? My therapist said I yell at him
                because he only takes me seriously when I yell. Yell too much,
you lose your voice. Bobby Seale was bound and gagged
        at the Chicago Seven trial, his lips separated
                around a cloth. Abbie Hoffman screamed "a shande
fur de Goyim!" at Judge Hoffman, using Yiddish
        because they reached the dead-end of English, because
                you can't gag a person and call the remaining language
free. I had to ask what it meant:
        you're making a fool of our people.
                When boys learned the aleph-bet in cheder, each letter preceded
a drop of honey on the tongue. Learning, the logic went,
        should always be sweet. The last time I saw my great-grandmother
                I waited until my parents left the room, and then,
in perfect English, said I loved her. She looked at me
        like I had my head cut off. Language loosened
                back to honey on my tongue.

Falls in Love, or Reads Spinoza

The latter falls in love, or reads Spinoza, and these experiences have nothing to do with each
other . . . these experiences are always forming new wholes.   —T. S. Eliot

I meet a man with the final line of Spinoza's *Ethics*
tattooed on his forearm. If all ink tastes like salt.
If the closer we get, the worse it grows. If in *Spinoza*,
Leivick writes in Yiddish "Me times me is—
you, near times near is—far," then I am far
from my father working
the motel night shift, yet I remember him reading
Spinoza over the hum
of the beer cooler, remember my father phoning
to say, "Spinoza says
we can't recall what we forget, or forget
what we recall:
we are not free." My father leaving dog-eared pages
of *Ethics* above the toilet
times Spinoza punished for having found divinity
everywhere, in the democratic
motel rooms where the saddest nights you can think of
pass for love. Then the things people do to feel
closer. Then my date shows me the door.
Then my father, dumped in school, stealing the girl's makeup
so she'd call. The phone ringing and her father
asking, "Murray, you plan on wearing her blush
or returning it?" If we don't choose
what we return. If we aren't free.

At the Laundry After

The orange cord slaps
against the concrete. The vacuum hits
the wall. His chest rattles
like the laundry, a birdcage bright
as fruit, hangers noisy as *ff*
penciled into the fresh, hot steam.

At the laundry after his wife died,
at the laundry after his wife died,
at the laundry after his wife died
like it could come out like a stain.

At the Ohio History Center, there's a cross-section
of a tree under glass. You can see Ohio's hardest
winters in its rings. I imagine looking at a cross-section
of my grandfather, museum-exact arrows
pointing to where a visitor
can see the death of my grandmother,

can see him circled by sons-in-law
around the holiday table until
he's fist, fist, fist—an argument mounting
in the topology of a mountain, a geology
piling up on the table without
regard to his third daughter's silver.

Once he was patient: he waited
with the others for information.
He was ready to leave
when a man came to him
and said, "Your father? Sure I knew him,
a funny guy! Used to shake up a can
of beer and pass it to some sucker
across the line."

There was money to be made on the line.
My aunt said: "I was on the assembly line
and my friend was working across from me.
The radio was playing—it was loud because it was
so loud in the plant—and the song
'Since I Fell for You' by Johnny Mercer
came on. We both looked at each other
and began to sing—as heartwrenchingly
and as dramatically as
a Greek and Italian can—to each other
across the line."

It's good humans do something heartwrenching
across the lines. It's good to cross them. Though take the bomb:
that's a bad kind of crossing,
but when my grandfather
tells his war story, it's the bomb that
saves him, that saves the Italian from Kentucky
who never saw a telephone
and pressing his ear to the receiver
screamed the devil was taking his head.

He was a three-stripe sergeant, very brave.
Now, to prove his bravery, he sleeps with shelves
of books above his head. "What
if they fall?" asks his daughter, his daughter,
his daughter, his daughter, his daughter,
his daughter. "And what if!" he answers
each one in good Greek.

After dinners the daughters take half an hour
to achieve every permutation
of saying goodbye—hugging and kissing
though no one's moved from town
in fifty years. But how to say goodbye to him, a man
heading the table like a god
in a button-up and lilac pullover,
with eyebrows across his forehead
like a Richter scale, a man so handsome
that it's hard to look
at his wedding photo—his black hair cemented
in the opposite direction
of his lust, each destroying the other
so he stands up straight and tall
in the basement of unfinished St. Demetrious
where his life is just beginning,
where a woman is moving toward him
in straight line, in a $10 dress.

The Marquee Is Empty at the Big Rig Saloon

                which used to be called Clover Junction.
All the turnover—my friend in Vilnius,
                her dad still absently says, "Turn right
on Lenin" and she says this
                is how people get lost. In the thick of names.
Back when the bar was the Clover
                it was a diner: the Motel Clerk smoked his morning cigar
in a sunlit booth. Now everyone's calling out keno numbers
                and well drinks except my father
who's drunk on half a Coors and saying,
                "If the mother didn't run after
her children into the fire,
                the guard would say, 'What kind of mother are you!'
and push her in." The marquee says nothing.
                The band covers "Can't you see
what that woman's
                been doing to me?" so he switches
from *17 Days in Treblinka*
                to the time
he watched the Marshall Tucker Band
                get stoned downtown. My mother pretend-spits
over her shoulder
                to rid the world of genocide
and hash. I was raised in a utopia
                above her shoulder. My father grew up at the trucking motel
next door. This afternoon, he paced the office
                and stared at the empty sign.
I said, "Don't worry,
                they'll make it." He answered, "How do people watch
their children burn?" Above the circle of truckers at the bar,
                there's an old motel sign:
OPEN 24 HOURS
                WE NEVER SLEEP framed by flat screens
showing the CIA torture release, showing highlights
                from the game: players rubbing their fingers

in Johnny Football's face. Outside, semi-trucks thunder down
        the off-ramp. The motel sign looms
high up in the weather. The sky fights
        for every inch
it keeps empty. The owner drops off
        the bill, says it's much too slow
for a Friday. My father jumps out of his chair,
        points to the empty sign
and says, "Goddamnit,
        you say you're open
or you shut up."

Silence

How long will you be silent, Almighty sadist?

—Isaac Bashevis Singer

They gathered around the silence. They wondered who should break it,
what to break it with. The holiest one, he refused
and they were glad of it. Can you understand this kind of gladness?
Like the relief of a cloudy day when you've been too lucky. Like luck,
an alphabet to break from. Rolling with poppy seeds for vowels.
We were taught it: silent aleph, silent opening: we practiced sounding it out
and broke into laughter. What quiet children! our teacher praised.
The chalk clicking against the waxed green board. Tree buds blowing
through the wall of open windows and scattering over the floor.
The silence lengthened by those who couldn't speak
in such weather. For lunch they gave us orange segments
and a question with many answers. One was forgetting.
One was our fathers' fathers, most of whom we never met.
Many of whom are silent. What happens when you call upon the silent?
It depends on what you consider an answer. Some said let the silence be.
Some talked over it until it became indistinguishable from listening.
Some said they were making too much out of it. Making too much
out of nothing? one said, slamming his hand on a table—the problem is
that we're making too little, not enough to get by! Maybe not for you,
a woman yelled back. I guess it depends on what you consider enough.
There are historic precedents. The holiest ones found this remark hilarious
but they were always fasting so it was hard to tell. They all faced east but,
with all their swaying, it was hard to tell.

Walking Far from Home with Charles Reznikoff

smiling up at me from my book, I am late
for a bus and know I will miss it
and need to kill three hours until the next.
I imagine Reznikoff happy—we get to walk more,
past Revere's grave, through North End's banners
of cannoli ads. Boston has the money to stay old—
in Youngstown, it'd be a parking lot. Back home,
people fight to save façades, or even bricks,
or even the thought of bricks. The only safe history
is in the steel museum
where, for seven bucks a ticket,
Ellis Island meets The Great Migration. A sign warns
"To touch may result in death"
in Croatian, Hungarian, Slovak. Owners discourage English
so workers don't unite. Exploitation speeds up
and assimilation slows down
until, walking through the exhibits,
I become one: a child of the Rust Belt
raised in a Little Greece
with everyone wiping my face
with a pani. I am of my home
as Reznikoff's of New York, the diaspora
he carefully stacked atop
his father's diaspora
then set forth across at street level: the altitude
my ancient uncle wandered alone, the first in his family
to leave Poland, so much older
than my great grandmother
she wasn't born. Who knows what he did
alone in the city, young, younger than me—
if Reznikoff passed him on those streets
he surely didn't notice him
among the Yiddish street signs without time
to lose, immediately advertising
and advertising.

The Heart of It All + A Free Beer

There are too many things set
     in Ohio. There is even a river. For a while
all we had were couches and tongue rings.
     Now, it's over. All married. Each time you turned around
to face the Torah I hoped you were looking
     at my ass. You weren't, and your brother wasn't looking
at my sister. We've recovered. She married.
     At many Youngstown weddings there's a cookie table.
Back home, having a long last name
     is like having a big dick, is like having a nice
cookie table. My five aunts made hundreds
     of Greek cookies for my sister's wedding.
My mother would make them for school, at Christmas,
     and I'd bring them in with her motherly note,
"Take out the clove! xo." After my sister's wedding,
     my mother packed up a box of cookies
and said, "Don't share them with anyone
     who won't appreciate them." My mother's nightmare
is someone eating Greek food without having
     an experience. Baklava is something
she has left of one experience. My cousin
     cries about a guy, and I say, "Good, no one likes him
anyway." No, I don't. I say, "Find someone
     who'll treat it like an experience." And if you do
and if he doesn't, forget about the clove.
     He'll ask, "Was I supposed to swallow that?"
Answer, "That's what she said." My cousin
     rolls her eyes, says I don't
understand. The time spent convincing the heartbroken
     you've been heartbroken. The last time I saw him
was in a Columbus library. We'd both left town,
     yet there we were: the back of his neck
in Literature, D-F. "I could not speak, and my eyes failed,
     I was neither living nor dead," are *Waste Land* lines
Pound wasn't allowed to cut. A hallucination?
     I emailed: it was him, he asked why I didn't say

hello? Because it's possible to stay too long
        at the fair. Because aisles over in L
was the Lorca
        I once watched a guy from Madrid
angrily re-translate in red ink. Even now, it's there—
        written and written
over. Even now, a Great Lake
        and a river. Things are set in Ohio
because you're allowed to stay too long
        and call it love. Because there are no
regulations. My mother waits up
        for my father who works at a motel
that never closes, that gives customers
        the heart of whatever they've come for
plus a free beer with every room.

Cleaning Motel Rooms at Night

17, a virgin, I clean motel rooms, stripping down
the beds, dumping ashtrays,
cleaning until desk, sheet, and Bible

fix in a trinity. I clean because
I'm the boss's daughter
surrounded by actual women

who clean for a living,
who call me "sweetie"
unless I'm wiping down

a door, unless I approach love
backwards, through its aftermath:
the threadbare comforter

slumping to the floor, the fit
of new sheets
taut as longing

across the bed. The room is ready,
waiting in the stillness
of an Ohio summer night.

I look back at the floral spread
and try to imagine a man
but cannot—

a clean room is a clean room,
a space straightening
endings and beginnings

into a line. To break it,
there's a price. Up in the darkness,
the rate flashes on the sign.

Another Dayshift

There is no before or after in the Torah.

—Rabbinic axiom

My father dials wake-up calls:
in the dark rooms,

ringing. I brew a pot
of office coffee and restock

beer. Outside the window,
the exit fills with semis.

We're sitting where
his father sat:

the window uses us
to tell the year.

The Great Bearer
of Keys

In the Back of the Motel Clerk's Mind, the Call Bell

The Innkeeper enters his office.
He's a 200-pound Jew in a leather jacket
holding a brand new call bell.
Business is good enough that he bought a house
and moved his family out of Room 1.
The turnpike is busy, the steel mills have ten more years.
He straightens up the counter, turns over
the bell and writes, "Bought bell 9/66.
In Bus. 6 Year. OK" He gives it a prominent position
on the desk. A trucker walks in
and asks for his regular room. The Motel Clerk doesn't answer.
He clears his throat. He points down at the bell.

The Motel Clerk Has Heard It Before

Truckers fantasize something tremendous. . . . I've seen fellas who build such dreams when they come into a truck stop they start to pour it out.

—Frank Decker, interstate truck driver

24/7 whiplash from being hit all day
by stories, a country's worth—   drivers, heads in hands, elbows on the counter,
          talking 55 mph
                    of endless night: double-nickel delirious

on cup after cup of truckstop coffee: the neon blinking   "How's Your Day?"
"my DAY? My god my day—hit my thumb dumb
          with a hammer and I'd
                    grin, good friend,

my day—"   and this at 4 in the morning, bleary: all day
people with days like this,
          years like this, the third time Chicago
                    to PA this week, in weather—   "Tell me did you ever stop

to think—There aren't enough pillows in this country
for my head—"
          the roads like this and their bones like this meteorological:
                    projecting, speculating, turned and overturned

then all emptied out
on the counter   the best minds left running
          overnight, run ragged through
                    the airwaves, the cornfields, through too much

and back again
to the Motel Clerk,   his wife, who spend their days
          listening behind the counter
                    like Deborah listening beneath the palm.

Night Portrait of a Motel Clerk

The '60s: a car hauler for every barstool.
A guy up the road has strippers out back in a trailer.
The roofs of diners slant up toward the moon.

The motel just opened: above it, a blinking arrow
casts its long shadow down the lawn.
The screen door opens

and a pimp enters the office, wet leaves violent
on his shoes. He tosses some cash
and ashes his Avanti on the counter.

The office is surrounded on all sides
by American midnight. The Motel Clerk
isn't sure what to do. He runs his eyes

across the repeating teeth of key rack
then tries, "Why don't you ask around
if you should *fuck* with me?"

A Conversation with America About Small Businesses

The line burns down,
the line goes bang!
—Vladimir Mayakovsky

The Motel Clerk signs another line
and puts a check in the mail. The line is a threat:
the ways to approach it. A pen or a fist, a pen or a fist.
The politicized space between the pen and the line:

the line of the fist, the fist of a name.
The will against. The will long dead
will heirloom, illuminate:
is a man sticking his hand in the wind

to say: *it is kite weather*. It is a day to throw things up in the air
and expect them to stay there. The line is taut,
is racing. America, please, more line. Please run your mouth
against his will in a textbook display of friction.

He signs and dates a check in a panorama
of liberty: a lady lifting a flame in the air,
the wind blowing smoke in his face
to say: *thanks for the light*.

Song of the Dead Office

מיט אַ בּגד איז מיר גוט

און אָן אַ בּגד איז מיר נאָך בּעסער.

I feel fine with a coat and even finer without one.

—Moyshe Kulbak, trans. from the Yiddish by J. Neugroschel

To rent rooms is fine and a dead shift
is finer—all those brass keys just hang there

so finely. A full lot is fine but it's fine
if it's empty—a fine sheet of snow

covers the difference. Time ticks finely
toward morning and away from the night—

the line between them so fine,
a line fit for signing. Your sign a good name—

a good name's worth a nickel—
a fine for having one,

a fine for forgetting. Finally you don't care
one way or another. Business is fine.

It couldn't be finer.

10-4

CBs spread the news across the interstate.
Semis lined the exit. Drivers stopped in to pay respects.
His sons stayed home from college to cover shifts.
It was winter. A new night clerk kept the vigil
of the night clerks.

But I break into your channel, O Daughters of Jerusalem,
to say the Motel Clerk left no myrrh
nor lapis for the fingers. He left a sign
that says MOTEL so big, no truck
can ever miss it, and compared to nectar,
are my songs of it not sweeter?

The Motel Clerk's Son Gets Bad Reception
of Cleveland 100.7 FM

Six days you shall labor and do all your work, but the seventh day is Shabbat for the Lord your God;
you shall not do any work.   —Shemot 20: 9–10

On a Friday night in the '70s, he takes over his father's shift
at the motel. He welcomes in the Shabbos
lighting a joint and turning the dial slowly,
ear up against the speaker, cracking
the radio like a safe. Murray Saul clicks, "*Cleve*land!
here's your weather. I went outside
and snorted the ground: don't waste your time,
it's fucking *snow*—" The ash hovers like snow
above the bottle. The snow hovers like ash
outside the office. Across the lot, the trucks
are running—the night's too cold to shut
them off—the engines circle themselves
for nothing. In the office, the radio pops
a word from its blister-pack. Through the static
fights Murray Saul, his voice surfacing
through the airwave's swell, until the lake effects
the state, until the words work Cleveland down
to suffix, to outskirts crackling with his words, their fat
and spit lifting up, up, up to Youngstown's static through which
he screams, "Ohio, tell your job goodbye—it's *FRI*DAY!,
and we gotta *GET DOWN!*" A commercial breaks.
He puts up the sign "be back in five."
Motel neon fills his father's chair.

Line Study of a Motel Clerk

Because a newspaper with hairy arms and practical shoes sprawls in
        the armchair behind the counter—
because a sign reads PLEASE RING FOR SERVICE and the yellow
        matchbooks WE DOZE BUT NEVER CLOSE—
because tonight, truckers all over the country aim their semis toward
        this clerk, this father asleep beneath the Business section
and because the ones who wrote today's edition have already written
        tomorrow's—
because right off the Ohio turnpike parking lots flower butt-ends of
        cigarettes—
because the doorway mezuzah is painted over and tough with
        weather—
because he's the great bearer of keys, the rack full of brass and room
        numbers, his mind the nerve-shot register and trucks still
        filthy with wilderness—
because in Room 1 his family sleeps, his wife wed fearless to
        business, *her value far beyond pearls*, their children
        dreaming in rows of doorframes—
because the truckers don't ring a call bell they mutter "Hey, Bill—"
        delirious, eyes stoned light blue from all the sky, from
        freighting speed all across the green summer—
because in this lobby one man's sleep is as good as another's

he wakes in a tent of letters and realizes that night's all around him—

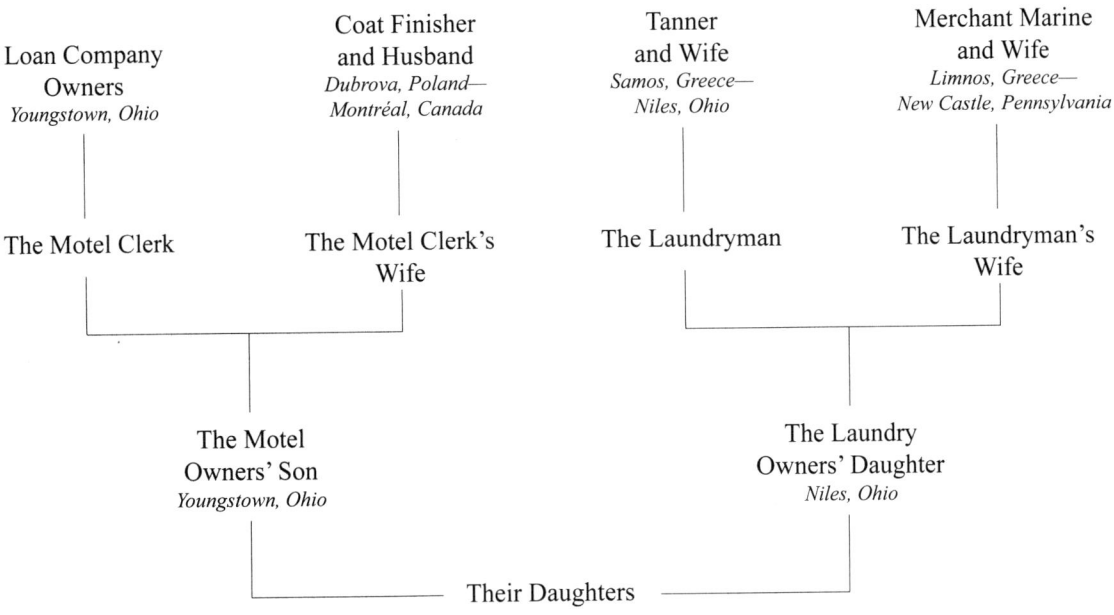

Loan Company
Owners
Youngstown, Ohio

Coat Finisher
and Husband
Dubrova, Poland—
Montréal, Canada

Tanner
and Wife
Samos, Greece—
Niles, Ohio

Merchant Marine
and Wife
Limnos, Greece—
New Castle, Pennsylvania

The Motel Clerk

The Motel Clerk's
Wife

The Laundryman

The Laundryman's
Wife

The Motel
Owners' Son
Youngstown, Ohio

The Laundry
Owners' Daughter
Niles, Ohio

Their Daughters

Notes

10. Epigraph: Nikola Tesla quoted in the *New York World-Telegram*, July 11, 1935. This poem and "Do we have any rock and rollers out there tonight?" are tributes to Left End singer Dennis "T. Menass" Sesonsky.

12. "When you have seven daughters, you forget to laugh, because seven daughters is serious business.": *Tevye the Dairyman* by Sholem Aleichem (1894), translated from the Yiddish by Hillel Halkin (Schocken Books Inc., 1996).

13. "Scoured the country for miles around / for milk and cream and eggs": *The Vindicator*, May 28, 1916, via *All Things Youngstown*.

20. Epigraph: John Berger and Anya Bostock's "Mayakovsky: His Language and His Death" (1975) from *Night Wraps the Sky*, edited by Michael Almereyda (Farrar Straus Giroux, 2008).

21. "Heave ho! My lads, heave ho! It's a long, long way to go": Lt. J.G. Jack Lawrence's "Heave Ho" (1943), the song of the Merchant Marines.

23. Epigraph: Harvey Shapiro discussing Reznikoff in *The Poems of Charles Reznikoff, 1918–1975*, edited by Seamus Cooney (Black Sparrow Press, 2005).

25. Epigraphs: teachings of Pythagoras and Louis Zukofsky's *A-12* (Jonathon Cape, 1966).

28. "The Maple Leaf, our emblem dear, The Maple Leaf forever!": Alexander Muir's "The Maple Leaf Forever" (1867).

30. References Henry Wadsworth Longfellow's "The Jewish Cemetery at Newport" (1854).

32. *Keneder Adler*: Montreal Yiddish newspaper from 1908–1988. Kalimera: Greek for "good morning."

35. Section title: Working back-to-back shifts when switching from night shift to day shift.

40. Title: Dalia Ravikovitch interviewed by Ayelet Negev.

41. For Barry.

42. "Co-eds called Guards motherfucking cocksuckers": *Kent State: What Happened and Why* by James Michener (Random House, Inc., 1971).

43. Title and epigraph: T. S. Eliot's *Metaphysical Lyrics and Poems of the Seventeenth Century* (Clarendon Press, 1921). "me times me is—you, near times near is—far.": from H. Leivick's "Two times two is four," from *Spinoza Cycle*, No. 11, (1932?). Translated from Yiddish by Ruth Whitman in *An Anthology of Modern Yiddish Poetry* (Wayne State University Press, 1995).

49. Epigraph: Isaac Bashevis Singer's *Enemies, A Love Story* (1966). Translated from the Yiddish by Aliza Shevrin and Elizabeth Shrub (Farrar Straus Giroux, 1972).

51. "I could not speak, and my eyes failed, / I was neither living nor dead": *The Waste Land* by T. S. Eliot (Horace Liveright, 1922).

54. Epigraph: a common translation of the Rabbinic axiom "En mukdam ume'uchar batorah."

58. Epigraph: Frank Decker interviewed in *Working* by Studs Terkel (Pantheon, 1974). Double nickel: CB slang for 55 mph.

60. Title and epigraph: Vladimir Mayakovsky's "A Conversation with a Taxman About Poetry" (1926). Translated by James H. McGavran III in *Selected Poems* (Northwestern University Press, 2013).

61. Epigraph: Moyshe Kulbak's "Montag" (1926). Translated from the Yiddish by Joachim Neugroschel in *The Shtetl* (1995).

62. Title: CB ten-code for "affirmative/transmission received." The poem references "Shir Hashirim" by King Solomon.

63. Epigraph: Shemot 20: 9–10. Quoted material loosely based on Murray Saul's *Friday Night Get Downs* broadcast on Cleveland WMMS 100.7.

64. "Her value far beyond pearls": Mishlei 31:10.

Acknowledgments

Grateful acknowledgment is made to the following publications in which these poems first appeared. In the case of alternate titles, the current title follows in parenthesis:

Black Warrior Review: "Falls in Love, Or Reads Spinoza."

Connotation Press: "Swings, 1970" and "Greetings from 41°6′0″N 80°39′0″W" ("Actual Afternoons").

Crazyhorse: "In the Back of the Innkeeper's Mind, the Key Rack."

CutBank: "Clarity" ("The Motel Clerk's Sons Take Over the Business").

Hampden-Sydney Poetry Review: "The Jewish Cemetery at Youngstown" and "Returning" ("Another Dayshift").

Missouri Review: "Inheritance," "Arriving in Canada," "Language Loosened Back," "The Motel Clerk's Son Gets Bad Reception of Cleveland 100.7 FM," "Dead Language," "Song of the Dead Office," "Greetings from the End of the Line."

New Republic: "Waiting in the Midwest" ("Cleaning Motel Rooms at Night").

Poecology: "Line Study of a Motel Clerk."

Sycamore Review: "The Heart of It All + A Free Beer."

"The Heart of It All + A Free Beer" was reprinted in *Best American Poetry 2016*, published by Simon & Schuster (2017).

"From The Back Room of the Laundry" and "Do We Have Any Rock and Rollers Out Here Tonight?" originally appeared in *The Youngstown Anthology*, published by Belt Publishing (2015).

"Arriving," "An Early Morning," and "What It Sounds Like from Here" originally appeared in *Poppy Seeds*, a winner of the Wick Poetry Chapbook Award and published by Kent State University Press (2013).

"At the Laundry After" originally appeared as "Mike Pitinii" in the *Jewish Currents Raynes Poetry Prize Anthology* published by Blue Thread Press (2013).

"The Motel Clerk's Son Drives Out to Check on Business" was published by Split This Rock as Poem of the Week on October 28, 2016.

While this collection references my experiences, the people, places, and events in these poems are often fictionalized amalgamations.

My gratitude to Ohio State University, the Wallace Stegner Program at Stanford University, the Fine Arts Work Center in Provincetown, and the Severinghaus Beck

Fund for Study at Vilnius Yiddish Institute, without whose support this book would not have been possible.

Thank you to all of my teachers, especially Kathy Fagan-Grandinetti, and to those who provided input on these poems—Henri Cole, Eavan Boland, and Ken Fields.

Thank you to Joanie Mackowski, Don Bogen, Tom LeClair, Jack Hay, and Vivian Axiotis McGarrity.

Thank you to my fellow writers, especially those who kindly read this manuscript at various stages—Kimberly Grey, Ari Banias, and others. Thanks to Curtis Vickers for seeking out my work, for your hospitality, and for your story about a father and son installing carpet.

Thank you, Baobab Press and Sundance Books and Music for being an inspiration to independent businesses everywhere and understanding where I was coming from—these poems found their home. This book owes much to the expertise and vision of the Baobab staff, especially Laura Wetherington, Christine Kelly, Molly Albert, Casey Bell, Margaret Fisher Dalrymple, and Travis Bennett.

My gratitude to writers and publishers exploring immigration and labor.

I have the kind of family where, if you run into your uncle downtown, he'll buy you a beer and tell you stories for hours. To a family that has its own haggadah, cookbook, play, and businesses—here's my addition. Thank you, aunts and uncles, especially Gela. Thank you, Marla, Suzanne, Laura, and cousins. Thank you, Ian. Thank you, northeast Ohio. Thank you, Mike and Betty Pitinii, Bill and Rhoda Davis, and my parents, Linda and Murray Davis. For generations past and future.

Designed by Baobab Press.
Author photo by Laura Davis.
The typeface is Clarendon URW and Times New Roman.
Clarendon URW was originally put out in 1845 by R. Besley & Co as
a heavy face to accompany an ordinary roman in dictionaries and the like.
Times New Roman was commissioned by *The Times* in 1931.
It is a newspaper type with short ascenders and descenders.
Printed and bound by Thomson-Shore Inc.